The Strength to FIGHT that Nobody Saw

Aquiashala S. Ware

BK Royston Publishing
Jeffersonville, IN 47131
https://www.bkroystonpublishing.com
bkroystonpublishing@gmail.com

Cover Design: Elite Covers

ISBN: 978-1-971868-25-7

Printed in the United States of America

Acknowledgements

There are so many individuals I could start off by telling you how grateful I am for them in pushing me to write this book, but I want to first thank everyone who ever doubted me. Thank you for the extra nudge I needed. Your disbelief in me put me down and had me in a dark space, but the lesson I continue to learn over and over is that no one has a say over my life besides God. And for that, I am well.

First and foremost, God I thank you for being YOU. It is because of you that I made it to this point. Something that seemed so far away yet was always in your plans for me. I thank you and I love you, Lord.

My husband, Cedric, has always been my number one supporter and is usually pushing me to step outside my comfort zone. With the process of writing this book, he did not have to push me at all. I went at my own pace and it all came out organically. Thank you, Babe, for believing that I can do anything. It is one of the best feelings to know somebody is truly in your corner and wants to see you excel. I love you, and we are only getting started!

To my children, Gabrielle and Skylar, Mommy is so head over heels for you it's crazy. You will never understand the fight it took to bring you into this world. But I would do it all over again if I got to be your mommy. You two are Mommy's best friends, and I believe in you to do great things. Have confidence in yourself, and manifest whatever brings your joy. I love you so much.

Table of Contents

Chapter 1

2013

The year of 2013 was a transitional phase for our family. We had sold our house and moved into a condo because we wanted to get out of the neighborhood that we were in. Our plan was to live in the condo until we established what neighborhood would best suit us and then make plans to start the process of buying our second home. Along with re-establishing our family in another area, my husband had been toying with the idea of starting his own business, to become a contractor for FedEx. He had worked for FedEx for several years prior to, so he knew how the business was run and thought he should give it a try, to see if there would be any success at it. Entrepreneurship had been something he spoke strongly about since we got into a relationship, and becoming a transportation contractor would help jumpstart some of his entrepreneur goals. Along with being self-employed, we brought up the idea of expanding our family. My siblings were nine plus years younger than I was, and my husband was an only child. Our only child, Gabrielle, was almost two and we wanted her to grow up with a sibling who would be close to her age. God had already planned for our family to make room for another child, because two months later, we received news that the Ware household would be adding another seat at the table.

I was confident with our OBGYN because we were going to go with the same doctor who delivered Gabrielle. Dr. Alicia Graves was a sweetheart. She explained everything so well, exuded an extreme amount of patience and, most of all, made me feel safe. The same uncertainties did not exist back then for me as they do when it comes to having to advocate for yourself during pregnancy. I felt heard from my doctor, and she listened to my concerns and responded appropriately. Meeting with Dr. Graves again at our ten-week appointment felt refreshing, because she genuinely cared for our family. She was excited to see us have more children and wanted to know how Gabrielle was and see pictures of how much she had grown. At the end of the appointment, she let me know she would be out for six-eight weeks due to a biopsy she needed to have done.

Apprehension immediately hit, and I asked, "For what?"

She said her doctor found a lump in her breast and needed to do a biopsy of it. Immediate concern rushed my face, and she grabbed my hands. "I'm fine, I just need to get it biopsied, and I am going to take a little time off, and I will be right back to see you at your next appointment."

How silly do I look, having her comfort me when she is the one who is going through a breast cancer scare? But I was nervous because I did not want anything to happen to her, and I did not want any random doctor delivering this baby. Of course, I assured her my family would be praying and everything would work out for her. Unfortunately, at our next appointment, we found out that Dr. Graves would remain off work until October. That lump she had biopsied was in fact breast cancer, and she had to start chemotherapy. Shocked was an understatement about how I felt. She was in such good spirits at our last appointment, and I could only hope she had the same energy to get through her treatment to overcome the cancer. The office let me know that a new doctor to the practice had been assigned to me because she was taking over care for some of Dr. Graves' patients.

Pregnancy went fine with Skylar. My weight was consistent. Her growth was right on track. My morning sickness was not as bad as it was when I was pregnant with

Gabby. We started the process of looking for a new home around April that year. I would say at around 21–23 weeks, I started to notice something weird occurring to me that didn't happen during my first pregnancy. When I would use the restroom, I would notice a discharge that appeared to be light green. No scent, no pain, and it happened only occasionally. I didn't pay much attention to it until it started happening every day. I Googled it, of course, and Google says it is common for women to have discharges during pregnancy. Okay, no biggie. I continued on. I felt good. Looked good. I had a big event coming up. My best friend was getting married, and I was a bridesmaid in the wedding, so I had a lot of preparation to do. I remember it being extremely HOT that day. She was marrying her college sweetheart at a country club in Richmond, Kentucky. The country club grounds were extremely beautiful and peaceful. The wedding took place outside and the building that let out to the area was where the bridesmaids were primping and dressing to get ready for the big day. All our dresses, shoes, accessories, etcetera were on the first floor, and makeup and hair were upstairs. Did I mention there were three flights of stairs? I was a big, pregnant lady on what felt like the hottest day in May, going up and down three flights of stairs multiple times! I was exhausted before the wedding even started. You know what else started to become a nuisance. The excessive discharges I was having that day as well. I thought it was because I was sweating more than normal and moving around more that day, but it got concerning. I knew my appointment was in two days, so I made it a point to write it down to ask the doctor about it when I saw her for my follow up.

Ced dropped me off at the OB appointment while he parked the car. As I was registering, the receptionist told me I was going to see another doctor today who was taking care of Dr. Graves' patients for a while until she returned. I was concerned because her leave was only supposed to be 6–8 weeks and now they were saying she would not be back until October! That meant something was wrong. I didn't like new doctors. I wanted my doctor because she was whom I feel comfortable with. I had a serious concern going on, and I needed to be able to talk to her. My new doctor was Dr. Brown, who was new to the practice. Of course, she walked in, and I got ready to walk back out the room because she looked like she just graduated yesterday, and I didn't have time to be a guinea pig for labor and delivery. So, she introduced herself and I was steadily texting Ced, trying to tell him to hurry up because Dr. Graves was not there and my anxiety was at an ultimate high. Dr. Brown was asking me how things were going and I let her know about the discharge; in a minute, she wanted to do an exam, of course. Great, my most favorite thing in the world. NOT. Anyway, she asked me to get up on the table and scoot down so she could start the exam. I was staring at the ceiling thinking, '*What in the world is she going to really tell me? Does she even know what she's looking at?*'

As she was doing the exam, she remained quiet. Then, she said, "Hmm, I can tell you something does not look right with your cervix." *Okay, what does that mean?* She said, "I'm not sure, but there is a growth there that kind of looks like a cauliflower." Again, okay. *What does that mean?* She continued, "I am going to grab one of the other doctors in the office who has more experience than I do, so we can get a second opinion.

She stepped out the room and I called Ced. "Please get upstairs now!" I told him.

He said, “Sorry, the parking lot was busy. I’m coming into the office now.”

Three minutes later, he walked in and I started blasting off, “Babe, she has no idea what’s going on. She said my cervix doesn’t look right and there is a cauliflower growth on it.”

My husband is a very calm-mannered person in high-stress situations. He, of course, is trying to have me be calm and gets his phone out and says, “Let’s just look it up on Google.” He’s typing in “cauliflower growth on cervix” and starts scrolling. Almost instantly, he’s like, “This is saying cervical cancer!”

???? How can that be? Cervical cancer? I didn’t really think much more about it, because at that point, I was dumb enough to think it was impossible to have cervical cancer while being pregnant. Dr. Brown came back in with another associate and she examined me. I remember verbatim she said she'd been an MD for seventeen years and had never seen anything like that.

So now, we were really getting frustrated. I looked at Dr. Brown and said, "My husband said it could be cervical cancer. Is this possible?"

She said, "Yes, it could be, and I'm thinking it might be, but I don't want to say anything for sure until we do a biopsy and get back some results."

Cool. Let's get this over with so we can see what's going on. The results would be back on Thursday and we had another appointment made so we could come back to the office and meet back with her. Three days felt like three months. I can't really put together the thoughts that were processing in my mind throughout those next couple of days. Of course, we had so many family members and friends to fill in on the situation and explain over and over what was going on. I think dealing with the idea of it being a possibility was so shocking to my body that emotions were non-existent at this point. I don't know much about cancer. I have never had anyone close to me go through a cancer diagnosis. More or less, I've never heard of anyone having cancer while pregnant. Or having cancer at twenty-eight!

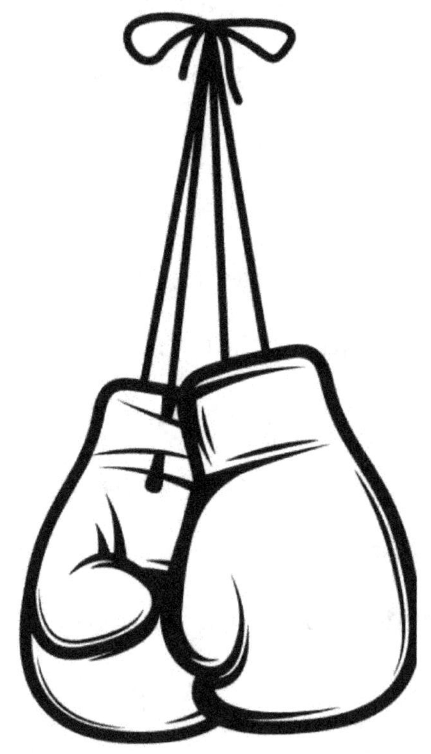

Chapter 2

The Results Are In

The results were in. I left work early that day so I could get to the appointment on time. I parked across the street so I could meet Ced, and we would drive over together. On the way to the appointment, he called me and gave me the great news that his contracts had been approved and he was officially able to expand his contracting business. I was so proud of him and so happy for him, but I don't know if I truly expressed it at that moment because I couldn't take my mind off what we were about to hear. I sat in the car for about fifteen minutes and called my Soror Tia. I needed someone to calm me down and talk me through my fears.

She comforted me and prayed with me and spoke words of encouragement. Ced pulled up minutes afterward, and we drove across the street and parked in the parking structure. Walking in, I tried to keep a smile on my face to show positivity, but inside, I was experiencing a different type of nervous that I've never experienced before. We didn't have to wait long in the waiting room, and Dr. Brown followed us into the room. There was no time wasted with the results, of course. I could tell from her face. I said, "It's cancer, isn't it?"

She said, "Yes, you have what's called small cell carcinoma."

Okay, the fears I had jumped up even more. The first wave of fear was moving up to my chest and I felt it starting to tighten, but I began asking several questions. I got right to it. “Am I going to die and is my baby going to die?”

She said, “No, you and the baby are going to be fine. But we do want to treat this before you give birth, and we are going to want you to have a C-section, possibly a little earlier than what you planned.”

“How do we treat this? With chemo? I can do chemo and it will not affect the baby?”

“Yes, but first, I want you to immediately go downstairs and get an MRI done of your pelvic area so we can see what we are dealing with. I also have made a referral to Dr. Milam, who is an oncologist gynecologist. I have worked very closely with him and he is going to speak with you about the plan of care from here. I have an appointment made for you tomorrow because we want to get started with treatment as soon as possible." Dr. Brown explained that I would also have to undergo a radical hysterectomy.

Ced and I both looked at each other and asked, "What does that mean?" I only knew about one type of hysterectomy and that was where everything was taken—uterus, cervix, fallopian tubes, and ovaries. But a radical was where they were just going to take my uterus, cervix, and some surrounding tissue. Okay. The tears were coming because I knew that meant we would not be able to have any more children. I was feeling like at any time I could wake up and this would all be over.

My husband and I went downstairs and registered for an MRI. The receptionist told us we had to pay $300 just to get the scan. I could already tell this was going to be a financial setback that we were not prepared for. I'd never had to do an MRI before, so I didn't know what to expect. My husband, who is a cancer survivor and had several MRIs as a young child, told me it would be loud, but they would try to play music to help calm me down. I don't think I was prepared with how loud it could be! I asked them to play some gospel music, and I'm not sure I could hear one song play, the MRI noises were so loud. Scary even. I was lying in this big machine for what felt like three hours. I could see people through a screen who were looking at me. Were they reading my reports already as I was getting the scan? I didn't know, but I was ready to go home so I could process how in the absolute hell I ended up in this situation.

The next day, I went into my oncology gynecology appointment. I looked around the office, and I tell you what, the oncology office was the busiest place you will ever see. But again, everyone I saw was probably sixty and up. No one my age. I felt out of place. But nevertheless, I knew I didn't really have a choice but to stay. I met Angela, one of the medical assistants, and she made me laugh and had a good aura about her. I like it when you can meet good people who seem to enjoy helping patients. We were taken back into the room where I met The infamous Dr. Michael Milam! To know him is to love him.

A gentle spirit who had eyelashes the length of *Mr. Snuffleupagus*, from *Sesame Street*. That was all I could focus on when he talked was how long his lashes were. He explained everything to me very thoroughly. Milam explained that the goal for my treatment plan was to shrink the tumor before I gave birth. Of course, he emphasized that my case was quite rare and "special", but he was going to help me through the process. The plan was for me to make it to 34 weeks and to have a C-section. And then minutes later, they would do a radical hysterectomy. Right now, they had my tumor measuring about 4 cm. He, of course, continued to ask me several questions about how I was feeling and if I was experiencing any symptoms. I told him I felt great, honestly, but was very confused about how this happened, but I just wanted to make sure my baby and I were going to be safe. During that visit, I also met one of the best doctors around—not just because of his research or how many patients he has helped take care of, but just because of his personality and passion for people. Sometimes doctors get a bad reputation for being uppity and careless because of the money they make and the stress they are under, but he far exceeded my expectations. Dr. Patrick Williams, my hematologist during this process, would explain to me about the type of chemotherapy I would be receiving. He showed me a study like my situation, where a woman was pregnant and received chemotherapy during that time. That was really the only research relative to my case that could be found. It didn't make me secure in my treatment plan but, again, I was "special", and I knew that I had to do what was best for me and the baby. I asked him when I would start and he said, "Monday." Umm, today is Friday, I have so many things I have to process before then, but whatever. I had to let my job know what was going on because there was a possibility, I would be going on maternity leave as soon as possible and would need to use all my PTO (paid time off) due to needing to start cancer treatments. But I wasn't ready to accept that yet and decided I would still try to work up until the surgery date. Later that day, I received a call from my insurance company, going over all my information and the call ended with them telling me that my treatment plan would not be covered. How is that so? They told me because there was not sufficient information that these treatments were necessary.

Chapter 3

Fired Up

I was fired up and already planned on being at the oncologists' office as soon as it opened because somebody was giving me chemotherapy whether they liked it or not. No matter the cost, I was getting this done because I was having this baby and getting rid of the cancer as well. We had to wait about two hours before everything got straightened out with the insurance, and we were seated in a room with an oncology nurse. I was educated about the type of chemotherapy I would be receiving and what some of the symptoms/side effects were. My number one question was if my hair was going to fall out. I was told it could or it could not, because everyone's body takes chemo differently. I had a little bit of hope that I would be able to keep my natural hair that I had been trying to grow out for the last year and a half. My husband reminded me that it was not important, though, because hair is hair. It's easier said than done. I also was given my schedule for what would take place. I would be receiving chemo Mondays from 8–5 and Tuesdays and Wednesdays for about two hours. Then, I would skip two weeks and come back again. I would do this until I reached 34 weeks, and then we would go into surgery for a C-section and radical hysterectomy. *Okay, sounds like a good plan from here,* I thought. I'm not a fan of needles, so I had to clench myself tight and stare at the ceiling whenever they decided to poke me, whether it be for chemo, labs, etcetera. But the first round was not so bad. I had a weird taste during the treatment, but other than that, I felt fine. As a matter of fact, my first week of chemotherapy was not bad at all. I thought this would be an easy ride. I would say I had bouts of fatigue, but my husband kept me pretty occupied so I didn’t let the fatigue take over. He even had me outside pulling weeds one day after treatment. He continued to tell me that we were going to fight this battle together so we could remain a family. Week two, I went in as normal to get my treatments and remained steadfast on my goals. Do what you got to do to survive and keep the baby healthy. My mom was in town helping me get adjusted, helping Ced and me with the household and making sure Gabrielle was okay as well. At two and a half, it becomes very hard to explain that your mommy is going through something right now, and that she's going to be in and out the hospital for a while. I remember it being a Thursday and my mom had to return home because she needed to get back to work. I remember she caught an Uber to the airport. I rose out of bed that morning and went to the restroom and immediately started bleeding. I knew I couldn't panic because Gabrielle was at home with me still. I was planning on taking her to daycare because Ced had already left for work. I called my friend and asked her if she could come and get Gabby to take her to daycare. Then I had to call my husband and my mom to tell them what was going on. My husband was in Elizabethtown, KY, running one of his routes, so he wasn't going to able to make it to me quickly. I thought about calling an ambulance, but my mom got our hairdresser to pick her up from the airport and swing around to the condo to pick me up. When I tell you she got to that hospital, it was less than ten minutes. Oh, my goodness! I went into the ER and was waiting for them to see me and decide what to do. My husband showed up about an hour later at the hospital. At this point, I thought something was wrong with the baby and that it must be the chemo affecting her. Imagine the kind of fear I had when I saw that bright red blood. The staff took me to get what is called a "picc line" in my arm. (It stands for "peripherally inserted central catheter" and is a tube that gives the doctor access to the central blood vessels around the heart.) On the way to the Xray room, I heard the infamous line I would hear all the time: "You're too young to be in this situation and have cancer." Really, really?! Ultimately, they determined it was just the tumor trying to shrink and that the baby and I were fine, but I would need to go on bed rest immediately. I hated that because I am not a person who can sit still and wait. It's never been me. My patience is not strong enough for that. So, I was going to have to sit at home doing nothing but daydream about how my head was going to look bald and if the baby and I were going to die. Not good for anyone's mental status. I had these emotions to process, only with the fact that in the hospital, my husband found a home for us to purchase. I had not been on the home search lately because of everything going on. But he showed me pictures and it had the space we needed, the location was perfect, and it checked off all of our needs and wants boxes. I was eager to get out of the hospital and take a peek. I was discharged from the hospital two days later and followed up at the oncology office. I had another scan done before this appointment. My mom went to this appointment with me, and the doctor told us both that my tumor had shrunk in half! He said everything was moving in the right direction and that I had a lot of people praying for me. That warmed my heart to know that someone was sending up an extra prayer to God for me.

Chapter 4

A Day Early

I went into the hospital a day early because our baby girl was going to be delivered early the next morning. I was feeling inspired and hopeful that night and knew this small trauma would all come to a halt once we saw her beautiful face. We got some visits in the hospital from family and friends and prayed with everyone and knew this, too, shall come to pass. I had to receive some more magnesium that night. Seems like I was always getting magnesium during this pregnancy, especially after the diagnosis. It's a running joke in the household that when Skylar is being silly, we say, "Oh well, it must have been that magnesium." The time had come for the baby to be delivered and for this tumor to leave my body. I was in the pre-op room getting all my vitals recorded and being prepped for surgery. I heard a familiar voice coming down the hall, and the curtain was pulled back. It was the same anesthesiologist I had when I delivered Gabby! I immediately burst into tears because God knew at that moment, I needed a familiar face. He was so kind and gentle when I got my last epidural. It put me at peace. I think any pregnant lady will tell you that one of the fears about delivery is the epidural. This doctor was great, and I barely felt a thing. He told me he would meet me in the surgery room and left. The nurses started to wheel me down to the room and my husband left the room to get his PPE on so he could come into the operating room. Dr. Milam and Dr. Brown were there and offered words of encouragement, and all of the nurses there at my side were so patient and kind, which was a huge relief. Despite the situation, I was so excited we were going to meet Skylar finally and so excited for us to be a family of four. My back was prepped for the epidural and in walked in the anesthesiologist. I am telling you, it was another successful epidural. As soon as he was done, I yelled out, "All of y'all make sure he gets paid first because he is the truth." Everyone burst out into laughter. I had to find some type of laughter in such a tense moment. My belly started to be prepped and iodine was rubbed all over. I remember asking Dr.

Brown to do a good job with my scar just like Dr. Graves did. I knew this time would be different, though, because I would have a scar that went horizontal for the C-section and then for the hysterectomy, an incision vertically would have to be made. I remember all the tugging and pulling I felt. No pain, just discomfort. Ced was talking to me to keep me occupied, and soon we met Skylar Noelle Ware. Born at 7:57 a.m. at 3 pounds, 14 ounces. So tiny and so precious. We held her for maybe a minute, and she had to be taken to the NICU, but they said was healthy and looked great. Ced kissed my forehead and had to leave and went to go see the baby. I had a long, warm float device blown up and felt warm across my chest. They told me I would be given medication that would put me to sleep and in 1, 2, 3 seconds, it was black.

***

NICU/ICU

I woke up in a regular hospital bed with a nurse named Ashley. Obviously, I was out of it, but as soon as I opened my eyes, she said, "Woohoo, you are cancer free!" She told me the surgery was successful and that I did great. In due time, I would be moved to a room, but they wanted it to be in ICU just because of the severity of what I went through. My care team felt that I needed to be watched closely. My memory was vague around this time because I was, of course, medicated for my pain, and so much had happened to my body in that moment.

But I vividly remember asking about who the baby looked like, and my husband was showing me pictures from his phone. Not the way I would want to remember first seeing my child, but I was too weak to visit her in the NICU, and everything that happened right before surgery was a distant memory at this point. But she was so small and so sweet. Our tiny little blessing. My parents were able to visit the baby, as well, and were reassuring me about how healthy she was and how everyone was so amazed by her strength. The next day, of course, it was on my mind to get out the bed and go see my baby! I could not walk yet, so my husband had to transport me via wheelchair. The pain was unbearable. I think I thought I was going to bounce back quickly, like my C-section with Gabrielle, but this surgery was going to hit a little differently. My husband wheeled me to the 3rd floor. You had to check in (yes, baby thieves are a thing) and then you go through these huge doors, and it's like a jungle paradise. The colors are so bright, and it's so quiet. Each NICU baby has what I called his or her own little "dorm room". I looked out over the nurses' station, and there was my baby on the end. I entered the room and I had no words. She was so beautiful and *so* tiny. I couldn't believe this gift God had given us despite all the circumstances. When I was in the hospital after the bleeding scare, a neonatologist came into my hospital room to discuss the risks of having a NICU baby and explained to me about the potential for her to have respiratory issues, developmental delays, vision problems, etcetera, etcetera. And here I was, looking at a perfect angel who the doctors said would not be in the NICU for long. All she needed to do was pick up some weight and be able to drink from a bottle. I'd like that doctor to return the $300.00 he charged for his 15-minute visit with nothing but lies! No, but seriously, that was a moment God spoke to me and I said, "I got you."

Chapter 5

One Week and Released

I was in the hospital for one week and was able to be released. It was a long road to recovery, trust me. I had a hard time walking because of the pain. Once I was discharged, my plan did not involve chemo anymore because the cancer had been removed. So now, my routine was going back and forth to the NICU to visit Skylar every day. Learning to become a mother again and taking care of myself, my husband, and my two-year-old was quite an adjustment. Learning how to care for a NICU baby was a difficult task for me as well. She was so small and could fit in the palm of my hand. It took me a while to ever change her diaper because I was terrified of hurting her. My husband jumped right in and wasn't fazed at all. He handled her with such caution and care, it was amazing and a blessing to see. I wanted Gabby to be able to see her baby sister, but she was too young to visit. So, of course, she always got lots of pictures to look through once I returned home from the hospital, but she still couldn't understand why her sister was not home yet. I don't even think I could explain well what was going on with me. She was only two at that time. How do you explain any of the events that had occurred over the last couple of weeks to a child that young? I couldn't process anything myself.

Looking back, I would say the best and saddest memory I have about Skylar being in the NICU were the same. There was a moment when Ced and I were doing chest to chest with her and the NICU nurse was in there. I wanted so badly to be able to breastfeed her, but I knew she wouldn't be able to latch on yet. She was still getting food through some of her tubing. I missed out on the opportunity to start breastfeeding immediately because the chemo needed to be out of my body for several weeks before I started. I was able to pump in the beginning, but most moms can understand, if you don't get that initial contact, it's hard for milk to produce consistently. The surgery and her being in NICU worked against us. I was pumping, though, and still was able to produce some milk for her that way, but she received donor milk as a supplement, to help.

The nurse in the room, I will never forget, Ms. Geri, had been a NICU nurse for years. I could tell she was hardcore but the sweetest ever. She said, “Go ahead and try to feed her now.”

I asked, “Are you sure?”

She said, “Yes, she will be fine.”

I slowly put her up to my breast to see if she would latch on and she did. She barely received milk, but tears poured down my face. It was the only sense of normalcy to this delivery that I had. Everything about this pregnancy the last couple of weeks had been so daunting and filled with specialists' appointments, long, drawn-out doctors' visits, and the unknown about my health status. This was the first time I actually felt as if I had birthed a baby and we had that mommy/daughter moment. I will never forget that and always appreciate Ms. Geri for encouraging me to try. To this day, we keep in touch with her and send pictures of Skylar.

My birthday is coming up and it happened to fall on the day of my follow-up appointment post-surgery. I was excited because I was going to get that stupid picc line out of my arm. It served its use, but now it was time to get out! Do you know how hard it is to not get something wet that's in your dominant arm? I had to become a bath person because showers became complicated, but today, I was going to get me a nice hot shower after it was removed. My husband and I went to Wild Eggs right before the appointment to get some breakfast. I glanced out the window, and it was so gloomy that day. The rain was coming down and with everything going on, I thought it would feel more like a celebration, but something didn't feel right. I didn't feel joyous. I didn't have that jazz in me that you get when it's your birthday. Why? I asked God to heal me, and he did. Why wasn't I happy? What was missing? I couldn't put my finger on it, but for some reason, I knew today was not going to be a good day. We took that infamous drive up to the parking structure. Floor 4. I got very acquainted with this parking structure, unfortunately. More than I liked to. I checked in and we waited until my name was called. Again, I scanned the room for someone who looked like me.

Nada. Mainly senior citizens. Of course, they continued to look at me and my husband as if we didn't belong, but I was getting used to that. The medical assistant called me back and obtained my vitals before getting us into a medical room. We waited patiently for Dr. Williams to come in to update us on how well the surgery went. In walked the doctor, and if you could have felt the darkness that followed him and the energy his body had, it would have instantly made you uncomfortable. Ced and I were both sitting in chairs instead of me sitting on the exam table/bed.

Dr. Williams asked, "How are you healing? How's the baby?"

I answered, "All is good. She is doing well. Growing and learning how to drink from a bottle. Other than that, no concerns. As for me, I am ready to get this picc line out and enjoy the rest of the day because today is my birthday."

Dr. Williams said, "Well, happy birthday! You are turning how old?"

I said, "Twenty-nine."

He replied, "You look like you're eighteen. You got you a good one," as he fist-bumped my husband. "Listen, I want to discuss some things about the surgery and the pathology report."

"Sure. Go ahead."

The doctor went on, "Pathology received your uterus, cervix and some laparoscopic cells around the vagina after surgery. And, of course, the tumor was removed and there were no more traces of cancer. But the laparoscopic cells showed minor spots of cancerous tissue inside."

I instantly got warm, my neck got tight, and I grabbed Ced's hand and squeezed it tight. "Okay, what does that mean?"

"It means we are going to have to continue therapy, and on the back end then complete some rounds of radiation. The type of cervical cancer you have is rare and it is aggressive."

And, of course, I had to ask the infamous question again, "So does this mean I could die?"

Dr. Williams said, "Unfortunately, yes, that is a possibility. This type of cancer could take your life, but that is why we want to be aggressive with it and make sure any remaining cells in your body are killed and rule out metastatic cancer as well."

Just like when the anesthesia hit me before surgery, everything went black. I fell out of the chair onto my knees. Screamed at the top of my lungs and hugged myself so tight, I about lost my breath. My husband and the doctor both jumped to help me back up, but I was inconsolable at this point. I could hear Ced saying, "Babe, it's okay. It's okay. Get up, get up, it's going to be okay," but I couldn't hear anything else besides I was going to die. I thought Dr. Brown said I was going to be fine, and now, here I am about to lose my life I feel like. The next twenty minutes were spent with Dr.

Williams drawing pictures on the paper of the exam table about how the radiation would work and how many more rounds of chemotherapy I would do. They were going to give me a break this week, but the next Monday I would have to start chemotherapy again. I would go Monday through Wednesday, with a three-week break in-between. I would complete a total of three more rounds, and then as I got to the last round, there would be two weeks of brachytherapy radiation and thirty days of radiation of the pelvis. I was going to be booked and busy, in a bad way, of course. After explaining my treatment plan, we were escorted to another treatment room where they needed to draw more labs. My mind went into overdrive and I began to throw out to my husband all the things that needed to be done. Because I was about to die, right? Coincidentally, we were supposed to close on our house that Friday. I told my husband we needed to call the owner of the condo and ask for an extension because there was going to be no way we could buy another home right now. And then I wanted to call the agent to let them know we wouldn't be going through with the house. Being an agent now, I understand that it would not be that easy. Cedric continued to plead with me to calm down, but there were so many things that I needed to take care of, and I might not have enough time to do it. As I was getting my blood drawn, my husband was calling my parents and his mom to explain everything that was going on. He texted the owner of the condo, and she responded quickly saying that she was sorry to hear what was going on with me, but she had already rented the condo out and we only had to the end of the month. Now, I felt that we had no choice but to move because where would be go with such short notice? We were about to close on a house, bring a NICU baby home, and have me start chemo again all in the same week. How was this even possible and how could anyone even function in these conditions?

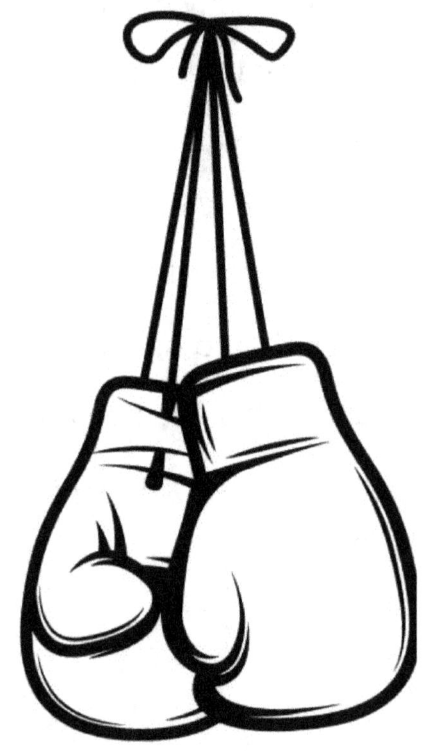

Chapter 6

House Closing

July 18th My mom flew back into town to help us move that weekend and accompanied me to the closing. My husband was working that day and had to sign paperwork quickly and then head back out. Gabby was at daycare, and my mom and I planned on seeing Skylar right after we closed. I am a realtor myself, and closing day is known to be an exciting time. But for me. Neh. This was another doomsday for me. Here I am signing papers on this beautiful home that we finally found for our family, but what good would it do? I wasn't going to be here long, was I? My life was coming to an end in my mind. The attorney and realtor stared at me in confusion, because with each paper I signed, a tear fell down my face. How could I help my husband with this house? Who knows when I would be able to work again? *So* much pressure on him that I didn't want, because this diagnosis and a NICU baby were already enough to deal with. Not to mention, the mental toll it could be taking on him as well. Not many know my husband is a cancer survivor himself. When he was a year old, he was diagnosed with a rare cancer called Histiocytosis X. in 1985, very few knew what it was and how to treat it. He had to endure radiation himself and had to see specialists at Vanderbilt University until he was fifteen. I can only imagine the amount of stress he could be under at this time, but he continued as if it was just another day. That weekend, he and my mom moved everything out of our condo and into the house. I had some friends come by and unload clothes for us, but other than that, my mom and husband got it done.

***

Bone Scan

With this new diagnosis, there were a lot more scans involved. PET scans and MRIs seemed to be my new favorite pastime. NOT! Have you ever drunk the flavored drink right before the PET scan? It is horrific! And they have the nerve to ask you if you want fruit punch or lemonade flavor. Neither—it's all disgusting! My chemo schedule started back up the Monday after my birthday, but we also had to wait for the PET scan results to determine if the cancer had spread anywhere else. With the cancer being a rare kind that spreads quickly, there was a fear that it could have metastasized and was in other places in the body. I was visiting with Skylar in the NICU and one of the nurses was with me. I knew they were getting ready to call with the results and I asked her to pray with me and to stay in the room with me. I didn't want to be by myself when I got the call. I also needed a medical professional with me, just in case I didn't understand some of the verbiage they used. I needed someone to break it down for me because I tend to shut down instantly, once I start hearing bad news. The telephone rang and I knew it was Norton Hospital because, of course, I memorized most of the numbers at this point. Sad but true. I answered and immediately put the doctor on speakerphone. The doctor explained the way the PET scan worked, by describing how the liquid I drank beforehand helped to highlight certain areas in my body and would detect if there were any areas of concern. Good news was there were no other spots in the body of main concern. Not so good news was there was a spot on my right tibia and left frontal part of my skull that were undetermined if they could possibly be a focus area. I would need to undergo a bone scan to determine if those areas would need to be included in my treatments. I felt that was good news. I really didn't understand at that point but later learned they thought the cancer had spread to my bones.

***

Hair Falling out

I completed my third round of chemo, and a couple of days later, Skylar was able to come home. My schedule had to change tremendously. The reality set in heavily that now, I must take care of a newborn along with managing my chemotherapy schedule. I couldn't have days of fatigue because I had to make sure my husband and my girls were taken care of. I had 3,000 square feet of a home that I needed to keep clean. Cook. Make bottles. Change diapers. Drop off at daycare. Be there for my husband. And complete cancer treatments. I could do this. I just had to create a new normal for myself. I could do it. I could do it.

I had been growing my hair out naturally since I became pregnant with Skylar. So, it was pretty thick and long, but I had yet to wash it since I started the chemotherapy. I would ask the RN each treatment if my hair was going to fall out still and continued to be told that it could or it could not. I had yet to see anything happen, so I was holding out hope. I decided to wash my hair and twist it up because I wanted to have some self-care time. So many changes had happened in the last couple of weeks, and I felt it was important. I stepped into the shower and let the water hit my scalp. Instantly, I felt like I was at a spa. I let my afro get nice and soaked with water. As I started to section my hair to put shampoo in it, I looked at my hands and it seemed as if I was shedding a lot, because they began to fill with small lumps of 4c curls. I didn't worry about it because it had been several weeks since I washed my hair. I continued to scrub my scalp lightly and took my hands from my scalp, only to find bigger clumps of hair in my hand. I yelled for Ced to get upstairs. He ran up to our bathroom and threw open the shower door, only to find me there crying as I began to pull my hair from my scalp. He quickly finished washing my hair and let me know it wasn't as noticeable as I thought and said he could take me to go get it cut if I wanted to. I hurried and finished cleaning up in the shower and we headed out to Bardstown Rd. where he usually got his hair cut. The barber sat me in the chair and asked me what I wanted.

In a low voice, I said, “Please just shave it off because it will come out, regardless.” He got his clippers and I saw big chunks of hair start to fall all over the barber gown that draped me. Then I saw chunks of curly hair hit the floor and I sat there in silence as the tears just flowed down my face. It’s easy for someone to say, “It’s just hair,” but I’m telling you, losing your hair with no control over it is a hard thing for a woman to cope with. It took him about fifteen minutes. I looked in the mirror. Disgusted. I hated who I saw. I looked like a little boy. I jumped up from the chair and went and plopped myself in the chair next to my husband like a little kid who just got in trouble.

He said, “You look beautiful, babe.”

I rolled my eyes. I figured he just didn't want me to feel bad about losing my hair because he knew how bad I wanted to keep hold of it. It was gone now, though, so I was crying over spilled milk.

Chapter 7

Depression

Losing my hair was rougher on me than I thought it would be. I had to get used to going out in public and became paranoid that everybody was looking at me like, “Why is her hair cut off?” I think, for me, it signaled the fact that I was actually sick, and I thought people would notice something was wrong with me. You know how you can tell sometimes that someone is going through a sickness based off their appearance. I felt that my baldness would signal that for some. I tried the wig thing, but that didn’t work. I wasn’t willing to pay $200 for a really good wig, and they were itchy anyway. Something about the possibility of it flying off in the wind didn't sit well with me, either. So, I resorted to wearing scarves over it. Of course, here I am wearing scarves in the middle of the summer, looking like a fool, sweating, but I just wasn't comfortable being who I was at that point. I started to feel a negative cloud come over me. I was down in the dumps every day. I started to have nightmares about my funeral and how I wanted to be dressed and who I thought would attend. I would look at my children and instantly cry, because I knew for certain I wasn't going to be able to see them grow up. I had to sign Gabby up for daycare and I wouldn't even put my name on the emergency list. I only listed Cedric as a contact because who needs to have their mom on there when she's about to die anyway, right? Every time my grandmother would talk to me, she said, "My prayer is that God allows you to see your children grow up." That was what I wanted as well, but I didn't know if that was the plan God had for me. I would call my daddy in the middle of the night and cry and tell him I didn't want to die. Some of my friends, I wouldn't talk to on the phone. Everything was just so hurtful. Why was I going through this? What had I done so wrong, to cause my life to be in such shambles right now?

Usually, my husband can talk some sense into me, but even he couldn't talk me down off of the ledge. One day, he got fed up and said, "Look, if you don't want to live for yourself, at least live for your family." He said, "Your life is not over, you still have a husband and two girls who are depending on you to fight for yourself."

I stormed upstairs and cried because no one understood what I was going through. Life was paused for me right now. My life was filled with constant appointments. Meeting with new doctors all the time. Hematologist. Radiologists. Oncologists. My second address was at the hospital. And if I heard one more person tell me I was too young to be going through something like this, I was going to scream. I thought I was too young, as well, but obviously not. I lay out on the bed and stared at the ceiling (my favorite pastime). I remember the curtains being closed, and inside the room, it looked like the sun rays were really red yellowish that day. I said to

God, "If you want me to go, just take me. I don't want to put any more pain on anyone nor be a burden."

At that moment, the phone rang. It was my Aunt Deborah. She wanted to call and check on me, to see how I was doing. I told her about how fed up I was with everything. She said, "You do realize I survived cancer, right?" I hesitated to respond but then slowly remembered that not too long ago, we were visiting her at University of Louisville hospital when she was hospitalized, and they discovered that she had liver cancer.

I said, "Yes, ma'am, I remember."

She said, "And I fought it. Hard as hell, but I fought it because I couldn't leave your

Uncle Mike by himself. You have a family that is depending on you to come out on top and you got to fight for your life."

"It's so hard, Aunt Deb. I'm tired of dealing with all this."

She responded, "Yes, I know, but who said life has to be easy?"

She was right; who am I to think that I don't have to go through anything to live? I need to get off my butt and quit whining, because I have to be thankful about where I am. If I hadn't even been pregnant, I wouldn't have discovered the tumor. They caught it early enough that it hadn't spread everywhere through my body. I had a baby at 31 weeks and 6 days who was 3 pounds, 15 ounces who had not one single issue when she was sent to the NICU. I have a loving and supportive husband who has been my side the entire way. A healthy 2 ½ year old who has no idea what is going on. Just wants to love on me and spend all day with me. Family and friends who have come through and helped like no other. What am I complaining about? I sound selfish. I see patients all the time in and out of the oncology office who do not look well whatsoever. I had to take a different approach and see this situation from a different perspective. Sulking all day, would only cause me to be sicker. It was time to make a change.

Chapter 8

Radiation and Brachytherapy

Before I started exterior radiation of my pelvic area, I had to do this form of radiation called “brachytherapy”. I know, weird word, but it was explained to me as a type of radiation that comes from a sealed source that would be inserted close to the tumor. In other words, they were going to put a cylinder shape tool inside of my vagina that would release radiation because it would be effective for getting to the cancerous cells close to the pelvic area. I would have to complete this for two weeks. I can’t tell you how uncomfortable it is to have a source of radiation inserted inside your vagina and the therapist asking you to remain still for two hours. Again, I had one of those 'stare at the ceiling' moments because who the heck comes up with this stuff? I questioned myself all the time if any of the treatments I was doing were effective, because some of the treatments that were suggested I had never heard of. But my familiarity with anything cancer related was non-existent. If it gets the job done, let's do it and move on to the next.

Radiation therapy was the most underrated process I ever experienced. I had no idea about what would take place and thought that beams would be pointed toward my pelvis, burning my skin. Wrong! It is the quickest appointment you will ever have. When you arrive at your appointment, you must change into a gown and wait to enter the treatment room. You lie on a table and there is a contraption there that is pulled over you that focuses on the specific area that needs to be treated. You are asked to lie still and not move for about 10–15 minutes. I would say lying on that table was the hardest part of my process. When I received chemotherapy, I could have someone accompany me to keep me occupied. My husband, grandmother, and even friends sat with me during my treatments to help pass the time. We would always listen to music, watch TV or just sit and talk. But when you do radiation, no one can be in the room with you, not even the radiation therapist. You are alone in a big room, in silence. What is my number one thing to this day I still cannot do? Sit in silence and have the time to think. The mind wanders and is a terrible thing when it does. Radiation really pushed my faith to the limit. I felt horrible, had constant GI issues, and remained fatigued. I thought it would be easy, but I should have known not to assume that. For a few weeks, my radiation and chemotherapy crossed over one another and I had to complete them on the same day. The amount of distress it puts on the body cannot be put into words. I wouldn't wish it on my worst enemy.

October 31, 2014. Accomplishment is an understatement. This is the day I finished my last radiation treatment. When I walked out of that treatment room, there was a big bell that they have all their patients who finish treatment ring, as a statement to say,

"I made it!" I thought it was cheesy when I walked past it previously, but when it came to my turn, I rang that bell so hard, they heard me well outside the office. I threw my clothes on, walked out the office door, and I *ran* down the hallway. I mean *ran*. It was like I was doing track again. This hallway was one of the longest I've ever seen, and I used to complain about the length because I would be tired and would have to go back and forth Monday through Friday. But this day, that distance didn't seem to matter. I sprinted down the entire hallway because I made it. I made it. Something that seemed like it would never end was over. I fooled myself. I told myself I would never be able to do this and was too weak to make it through. But I was wrong. I beat myself up for so long and counted myself out. But it didn't take much to come out of it. It literally took the faith of a mustard seed that God would work it out for me. That's it. Once I started to believe in that, each day, as rough as it was, seemed to skip by a little faster.

Chapter 9

After Effects

My experience through treatment sounds scary and, yes, was very traumatic.

What scars have I been left with? One of the constant things I hear is you don't look like you have had cancer, even though I don't know what someone with cancer is supposed to look like. Every cancer patient does not look the same, because there are different treatments that affect them differently as well. One of my marks from treatment is my hair. Yes, I lost all my hair. Bald as bald can get. I got real acquainted with my scalp. My hair did not start to grow back until about two months after my chemotherapy was over. But there was a section of my hair that took longer to grow back because of where the radiation occurred on my skull. We used to joke and say that I had a football helmet on because of the design in my hair it created as my hair slowly grew back. Now, that section of my hair is a completely different grain than the rest of my hair. I call it my chemo curl. It is my mark, to remind me of how I acted a fool when I cut my hair off and thought I would be bald forever. Those horror stories that you hear about radiation and how it burns your skin. Thankfully, I didn't experience that skin discoloration, but because the radiation was focused on my pelvis and I had the brachytherapy, it shrank the walls of my vagina. I had to actually go to physical therapy to stretch the walls of my vagina. I laughed when my oncologist suggested it. Therapy for your vagina? Well, it is a thing and it actually was a pretty busy office as well. One of the most uncomfortable situations I've ever been in and something I could not wait to complete. Hot flashes have been a family member that I cannot get rid of. It makes me feel really old, complaining about getting hot flashes. But my body was feeling menopausal, with my cervix and uterus gone. It's something that will never go away. Every night, I am met with my little forty-five-second hot flash that jumps out at you in the most inconvenient time of your day. I have found ways to cope with it, and of course, a ceiling fan in a room is golden to me. Having more biological children is out of the question now, but adoption was an option for our family. As heartbroken as I was about not being able to give my husband more children, I'm so thankful God choose me to bring two of his children into this world. If you are wondering if Skylar ever experienced any complications from being born early, receiving chemo while she was still in my womb and even post labor, the answer is absolutely not. She is now eleven years old and is the most talented kids you will ever meet. She hit every milestone that the doctors said she would not be able to do on time. No respiratory, feeding, or developmental problems. As a matter of fact, she's the best speller in her class and can eat a chicken wing quicker than anybody I know. She fights hard and trains completely in gymnastics. Just seeing her be fearless and determined, makes my heart smile because she is a true walking definition of how miracles happen every day.

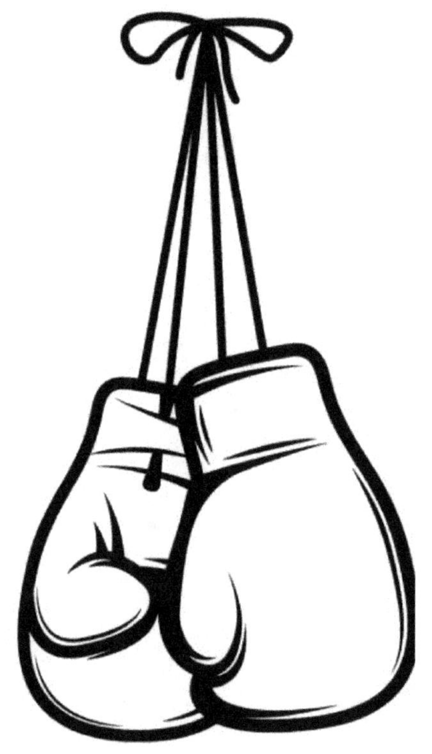

Conclusion –What I learned

Seven motivational pieces that kept me and that are still useful to this day.

1. My life is in your hands. I don't know if you have ever heard that song before, but it's by Kirk Franklin. The words are, "No matter what may come of it, my life is in your hands." This song was sung at my grandfather's funeral. He passed from a battle with cancer three months after I was diagnosed. This song was played toward the end of the funeral, and after listening deeply to the words, it was like a lightbulb went off and I continued to repeat the words over and over. My life was in God's hands. No

matter how much chemotherapy I received. No matter how sad or depressed I had become. No matter the circumstance. My outcome had already been determined for me and it was out of my control. I could either snap out of it, live whatever life I had left, or continue to sink into this sunken world of defeat and lifelessness. My family didn't deserve that, and I knew I had to turn things around.

2. What's for me is for me; what's not, I can't worry about it.

3. Never ask, "Why me?" Why not you? Who are we to question why something happens to us? We are no better that our neighbor. Trust me, the battle to process this fully took a long time for me. I had to quit being selfish and check myself.

Was my situation ideal? Absolutely not! Could it be worse? Heck, yes! My story could have ended another way. God saw fit for me to endure this and knew I would be able to defeat what doctors didn't think I could.

4. The saying is true. Go through any type of sickness or hard times, and you will truly see where your true family and friends are. I think they say the same thing about weddings and funerals, too, right? It's the truth, though. I learned who was actually going to stick to the statement of, "I'm here for you if you need me." My mother-in-law and grandmother came down every single week, Monday through Thursday, to help watch the children while my husband took me back and forth to appointments. My mother and father would then fly up from

Atlanta to Louisville, KY, Friday to Sunday, and do the same. I never had to worry about cooking, laundry, nothing. They picked me up at a time when I was lost and didn't know what good I was as a mother and wife. For that, I will forever be grateful to them. I had friends visit and sit with me at chemo or visit me at home, to see how I was coping with everything. My best friend came down one time just to twist my hair. I know she saw my hair was coming out and I was going bald from the chemo, but she didn't say one word. She washed and combed my mane as if I were at a personal salon and made me feel a bit of normalcy that I had lacked for so long. You want to test how strong your relationships are? Go through a storm in your life and you will quickly see if others stand in the rain with you or will they run to quickly get an umbrella to cover themselves.

5. Please don't complain about your situation. Know that someone is worse off than you who is struggling to get by. Watch the words that come out of your mouth, because the tongue is a powerful thing. You want to complain about your house being too small. Most people would die not to sleep on another concrete sidewalk. You want to make a fuss about there being too many items in the fridge. Shut up and organize it. Somebody is thinking about what they will have to do next to get their meals for the day. I'm not perfect by any means, but I am a true believer that what you think about, you will become, unless you change your own scenario.

6. I'm not trying to be a grim reaper, but let's be honest. Who would have thought that, at the age of twenty-nine, a perfectly healthy pregnant woman would end up diagnosed with cervical cancer at the same time. The odds of it seemed almost impossible. With that being said, stay ready as best as you can. Buy life insurance. You never know what could happen within the next five minutes. You want the ones you trust to be informed about how to best respect your wishes when you leave this Earth. Stop waiting until the moment you feel is best to make a move in your life. You only get one. If you fail at something, who cares? The fact that you tried to be different will be respected more than anything.

7. You create the energy that surrounds you. If it's negative, check yourself first. If the people around you are negative, remove them from your space. You only get one life, why spend it without faith, love, and peace?

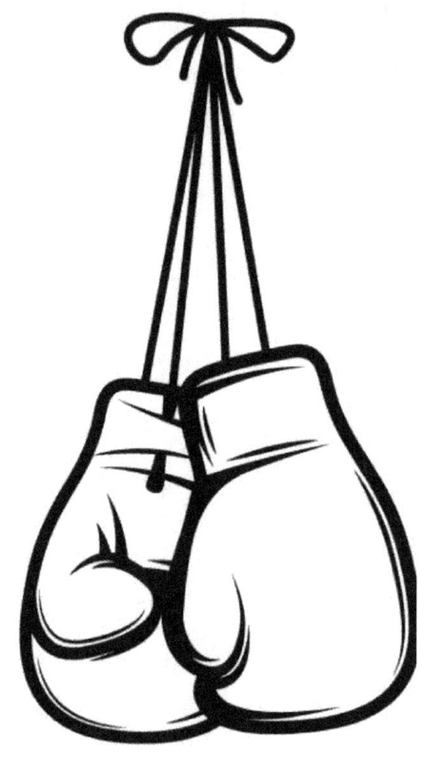

Scriptures for Strength

Isaiah 53:5

"But he was wounded for our transgressions, he was bruised for our iniquities: the chastisement of our peace was upon him; and with his stripes we are healed."

Revelation 12:11

"And they overcame him by the blood of the Lamb, and by the word of their testimony;.."

Faith

Habakkuk 2:4

"Behold, his soul which is lifted up is not upright in him: but the just shall live by his faith."

Matthew 9:29

"Then touched he their eyes, saying, According to your **faith** be it unto you."

Matthew 17:20

"And Jesus said unto them, because of your unbelief: for verily I say unto you, if ye have faith as a grain of mustard seed, ye shall say unto this mountain, remove hence to yonder place; and it shall remove; and nothing shall be impossible unto you."

Mark 5:34

"And he said unto her, Daughter, thy faith hath made thee whole."

Mark 11:22

"And Jesus answering saith unto them, Have faith in God."

2 Corinthians 5:7

"For we walk by faith, not by sight."

Galatians 3:11

"But that no man is justified by the law in the sight of God, it is evident: for, the just shall live by faith."

Healing

Psalm 30:2

"O Lord my God, I cried unto thee, and thou hast healed me."

Psalm 103:3

"Who forgiveth all thine iniquities; who healeth all thy diseases;"

Jeremiah 17:14

"Heal me, O Lord, and I shall be healed;"

Matthew 8:7

"And Jesus saith unto him, I will come and heal him."

Matthew 9:35

"And Jesus went about all the cities and villages, teaching in their synagogues, and preaching the gospel of the kingdom, and healing every sickness and every disease among the people."

James 5:16

"Confess your faults one to another, and pray one for another, that ye may be healed. The effectual fervent prayer of a righteous man availeth much."

2 Chronicles 7:14

"If my people, which are called by my name, shall humble themselves, and pray, and seek my face, and turn from their wicked ways; then will I hear from heaven, and will forgive their sin, and will heal their land."

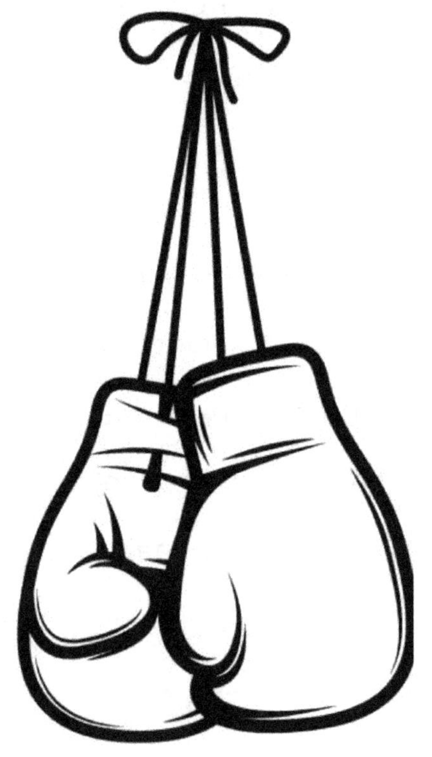

Prayer Journal

Prayer Journal

Prayer Journal

Prayer Journal

Prayer Journal

Prayer Journal

Pictorial Reflection

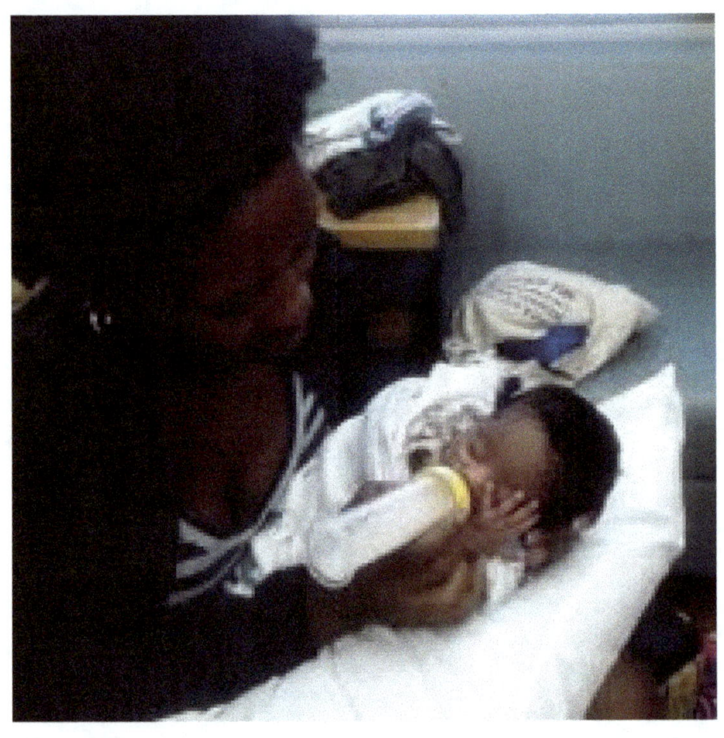

About the Author

Aquiashala S. Ware was born and raised in Lexington, Kentucky, and is a proud graduate of the University of Kentucky. She has resided in Louisville, Kentucky since 2010, where she lives with her husband of fifteen years, Cedric Ware, and their four children.

A cancer survivor, storyteller, and community leader, Aquia is a serial entrepreneur who has built a life rooted in resilience, faith, and purpose. She is a licensed real estate professional serving clients across Kentucky, Indiana, and Ohio, as well as an associate appraiser and the owner of a security services business. Throughout the week, she can be found writing contracts, negotiating deals, and guiding families through some of the most important decisions of their lives.

Evenings and weekends are reserved for what matters most...family. Whether she's on a volleyball court, in a gymnastics arena, or standing on the sidelines of a soccer field,

Aquia is fully present, cheering on her children as they pursue their passions and dreams.

A wellness enthusiast at heart, Aquia values physical and mental health and enjoys the gym, massages, facials, and intentional self-care. She loves to travel and prioritizes quality time, especially date nights with her husband. A devoted supporter of women's sports, she never misses an opportunity to watch elite competition and is especially fond of South Carolina and LSU women's basketball, while secretly hoping one of her children will someday pick up tennis or softball.

Aquia made a conscious decision not to let her circumstances define her future. Writing this book marked the first step in reclaiming her narrative and transforming survival into testimony. Through her story, she hopes to encourage others—especially women—to advocate for their health, trust God through uncertainty, and believe that even the darkest seasons can still produce purpose.

Today, Aquia continues to build businesses, raise her family, and use her platform to empower others through faith, perseverance, and community impact. While her journey is not something she puts behind her, it serves as a constant reminder that healing is ongoing, strength is cultivated, and survival is not the end...it is the beginning of something greater.

www.ingramcontent.com/pod-product-compliance
Lightning Source LLC
LaVergne TN
LVHW010613110826
845149LV00003B/896

* 9 7 8 1 9 7 1 8 6 8 2 5 7 *